MACH 4®

Mental Training System

A Handbook for Athletes, Coaches and Parents

Anne Smith, Ph.D.

MACH 4® Mental Training System

Published by Team Alf Books
Phoenix, Arizona

Phone: 480-272-5085
Fax: 480-214-5232

ISBN 0-9778958-0-7

E-mail: anne@annesmithtennis.com
www.annesmithtennis.com

Cover and Interior Design by Sential Design
www.sentialdesign.com

Front cover photo by Bev Raws

Additional Resources by Anne Smith:
MACH 4 Mental Training System (video)
GRAND SLAM: Coach Your Mind to Win in Sports, Business and Life (book)

What Coaches and Players are saying about the MACH 4® Mental Training System

Excellence with simplicity is the word that comes to mind when I devoured Anne Smith's MACH 4 mental training. I have read Jim Loehr and many others and this is by far the best and most simple method ever. The bible of mental training, she addresses the process of development and not the destination. The educational range with customization for personality types with increased personal development and effectiveness with tennis the goal. I have personally seen increases in mental proficiency with increases in skill or drill level difficulty. She has definitely met the challenge of increasing success and confidence by developing a training plan that works. The key is it works for every level of player & sport from beginner to advanced and that is the miracle and genius of her and Bev Raws' system. The plan is simple mental proficiency, learning behavior/ skills, experiment and practice, execution and follow-up with review. Why not mentally train while you are physically training? I have personally benefited and thank God for this revelation in mental training and personal development.

Mike Van Zutphen, Head Pro at Mesa Country Club in Mesa, Arizona, USPTA Master Professional, 4 time SWPTA Professional of the Year, 2 time SWPTA Coach of the Year, 2 time Recipient of USTA Community Service Award, USPTA National Tester

MACH 4 helps me to control my emotions and to concentrate on the court when I am playing. It has helped me to know when I need to raise my energy in matches and how to act like a champion. I have started to feel myself stronger on the court. MACH 4 has also helped me in my life. I am now nicer to people who are around me.

Oksana Kalashnikova, Republic of Georgia, 2005 16 & Under ITF Orange Bowl Champion, 2006 Israel ITF Junior Tournament 18 & Under Singles and Doubles Champion, 2006 Alex Podolsky ITF Junior Tournament 18 & Under Singles and Doubles Champion, 2006 ITF Junior Ranking #173 in the World

After we started doing MACH 4, I now feel stronger on the court. My groundstrokes have become better even though my technique is the same. Now I can win matches more easily than before. Using MACH 4, I don't waste my energy and I do not feel as tired after my matches as I did before. Now I'm more relaxed and not so nervous during my matches. I started to believe in myself. Everything got better with MACH 4, my technique and mental part of my game. I concentrate more in my matches which is why I pick up quicker where the best spots are to hit my shots. My serve got better as I've started to use cues before each serve. I just want to say that with MACH 4, I've started to think different and every part of me and my body got much stronger which is why the results of my play are so much better. Now I have such a feeling that nobody can beat me and I have more fun when I play.

Maria Kalashnikova, Republic of Georgia, 2006 Israel ITF Junior Tournament Doubles Champion, 2006 Alex Podolsky ITF Junior Tournament 18 & Under Singles Runner-Up and Doubles Champion, 2006 ITF Junior Ranking #402 in the World

When I started to do MACH 4, everything was getting better and better. It does not matter if I am winning or losing, I stay strong mentally and keep trying to be better. MACH 4 even helps me off the court. I never did it before and I like it very much. When I am doing my intensity 3, 4 and 5, I am not wasting energy and I am winning my matches easier.

Giorgi Khmiadashvili, 2005 Republic of Georgia National 14 & under Champion

I think the MACH 4 Mental Training System is a good way to improve the mind aspect of the game. It helps me to understand my temperament and to control my emotions better on the court. Since the difference between players at high levels is very small, the mental part is one of the most important parts to train. This will make the difference between the best players in the world and the others. MACH 4 also helps me to find the best level of intensity that I must use during the whole match. I now understand the reasons why I have had so many ups and downs during my matches.

Pierre Duclos, #4 in Canada, 2005 ATP Men's Pro Tour Ranking #675 in the World

MACH 4 has helped me very much in my practices and match play. I can now control my emotions, my body language is better and I am much more focused on the court. Since learning MACH 4, when I play, I am not thinking about winning or losing. I talk more positive to myself and I am now not afraid to miss shots. Opponents will not see any weaknesses from my actions as I must always be like a champion. I do not get upset anymore. I play with the same intensity as I practice. With MACH

4, everything has gotten better, on and off the court. I am very happy with this.

Salome Chachkhunashvili, 2004 Republic of Georgia Junior 16 & under Champion

When I just started to learn and use MACH 4, I knew it would help me so much. I know emotional control is very important in tennis and in life. If you want to be the best player in the world, you need to be strong on the outside and inside. On the court and in life, you have to be ready for everything. When I practice now, I do not fight with myself when I miss. I go on to the next ball and try to fix the problem. I look for more ways to be a problem for my opponent, not me. MACH 4 has helped me be a stronger player. It has also helped me be a good person with others. When there is respect in communication, there are fewer misunderstandings with each other. MACH 4 helps me live easy.

Anastasiya Kharchenko, 2004 Ukraine 16 & under Champion, 2005 ITF Junior Ranking #559 in the World

MACH 4 helps me to control my emotions. After I started doing MACH 4, I can now understand my play and my opponent's much easier. It teaches me I must have intensity 3, 4 and 5 during my whole match so when I am up in the score, my intensity will not go down which has caused me to start losing. Low intensity made it hard for me to win the match. When I think my opponent isn't as strong and my intensity would go down, MACH 4 taught me how to focus and get my intensity back. Since we do MACH 4 in our practices, it has helped me to focus in my practice time, too.

Magda Okruashvili, 2005 Republic of Georgia Cup 16 & under Champion

MACH 4 has taught me many things, how to help myself and how to become mentally and physically strong. Before I started doing MACH 4, I judged myself negatively. Now, I use cues and talk positively to myself. It has made me more aware of my game and how to improve my play. Right now, I am recovering from an injury and MACH 4 has really helped me with that. When I am sad or start feeling sad about not being able to play, I use cues such as what I will do after my cast is off or what I will do when I start playing tennis again. I can say that with MACH 4, I got better mentally and physically so this means I have become a better athlete.

Tatia Mikadze, Republic of Georgia, 2005 WTA Women's Pro Tour Ranking #559 in the World

MACH 4®
Mental Training System
Table of Contents

Introduction

The MACH 4® Mental Training System is a fast, fun, easy, effective way to teach athletes, coaches, and parents how to develop a prescription to win, increase self-esteem and confidence, control destructive emotions such as fear and anger, learn dynamic strategies for creating a positive learning environment, find effective ways to reach their maximum potential, allow themselves to win, and develop healthy, positive relationships that foster a winning atmosphere. Why call the System MACH 4? There are four components: mental, body language, intensity level, and cueing language. Combining these four components will help anyone reach their goals "faster than the speed of sound". MACH 4 is unique because it teaches how to develop empowering relationships between parents, coaches, and players, and how to create a powerful partnership between the mind and the body by highlighting the mind/body connection, focusing on training the mind and the body at the same time, and integrating mental training into practice sessions. If you are looking for something to give you that added advantage, MACH 4 is for you.

MACH 4 teaches much more than enhanced athletic performance. Life becomes easier, more rewarding and more fun using the MACH 4 techniques. Everyone can learn how to empower themselves and others by creating the best win-win situations. Using the MACH 4 System, athletes maximize their performance in sports by relating to specific intensity levels and by managing their emotions.

Winning can never be guaranteed, but we guarantee that if you practice using MACH 4 every day in and away from your athletic arena, you will enjoy life and competition more, and you will be more successful in relationships and all endeavors that are important to you. Your life and performance will become easier and more fun.

MACH 4 teaches you how to manage your emotions, which will improve everything in your life. Every moment of the day, events occur where decisions must be made and interactions with others become critical. MACH 4 ensures the best results at all times. What you choose to think in a moment, how you choose to act in a moment, and what you choose to say in a moment become defining. These three actions are all we really can control in our lives. Take the concepts from MACH 4, apply them not only to sports, but to relationships and life events, and you will be amazed at the positive results.

The mental part of the game is considered by most athletes and coaches to be at least 80–90%. Yet very few athletes and coaches take the time to train the mind at the same time they work on the physical skills of the game. If this mind/body training does not happen, how can the physical and the mental come together during competition? Mental training is about educating your athletes; just like you teach them technique, you can teach them mental skills to help them perform more easily and effortlessly with less chance of injury.

Most coaches only focus on technique and physical conditioning. Why not focus on creating mentally strong athletes who can perform when it counts? Mental training is the quickest way to improve performance. When players and coaches take responsibility for emotional and mental training, then they will have the complete package.

As an athlete, do you want to consistently perform your best, see immediate positive results, increase your confidence, control emotions that cause you to lose, be mentally and physically stronger, improve your concentration, and have fun and learn? As a coach, do you want to learn how to teach mental toughness skills, help your players perform better under pressure, integrate mental training into practice sessions, increase your player's self-esteem and confidence, identify thoughts and behaviors that hold your players back, manage team relationships, and improve team chemistry? If your answer is yes, then the MACH 4 Mental Training System is for you!

How do I know about performing and winning? From the time I was a teenager, I was among the most talented tennis players in the world. When I was 17, I was the first American ever to win the French Open Junior Singles Championships. Between 1980 and 1984, I won 10 Grand Slam championships in women's and mixed doubles, including three US Open titles, two Wimbledon titles, four French Open titles and one Australian Open title. I played with and against some of the greatest names in the history of tennis, including Martina Navratilova, with whom I won the French Open doubles championship in 1982. I was ranked as high as #12 in the world in women's singles.

Now, at age 45, I am making a comeback to professional tennis. I am playing singles and doubles on the International Tennis Federation (ITF) pro circuit. People have asked me why I don't just play doubles. It's because playing singles is a bigger challenge. Besides, my highest singles ranking was #12 in the world and that's not bad! Even though I won three singles titles, I firmly believe that if I would have had the MACH 4 System when I first started playing tennis and used it throughout my career, I would have won many more.

The game has changed significantly since I last played competitively in 1991. There is more of an emphasis on power now even though when I played against Monica Seles, she could hit the ball as hard as any of the current players. But, the game is about so much more than hitting the ball! All of these young women can hit the ball well. It is about the mental part of the game. This is where I benefit from what I learned studying for my Ph.D. in educational psychology. I have had to create a mind set that allows me to compete with players who are 20 years or more younger. These players work on the physical part of the game, but few work on the mental part. Most players do not even realize that it is possible to develop a tougher mental attitude much less about how to actually do it. As I have said to some of the players, "It's just like practicing a backhand down the line". Mental toughness can be learned. I learned it, so I will share with you how you can become mentally stronger so that you can win.

On this tour, I have seen many negative interactions between coaches/parents and players. It is very disheartening to hear coaches and parents speak in a harsh and derogatory manner to their players – their sons and daughters. They also foster dependent relationships that do not instill self confidence, self discipline, or self motivation. Time after time, I see players looking to their coaches or parents after every point. This does not create a winning environment. This type of support to a player just creates more stress and more reasons to lose. The job of a parent or coach is to find the best ways to enhance the player's performance. Through experience I know that a harsh, critical approach does not work.

It leads to self doubt, anger, illness, and injury. Players need a strong, supportive team to help them maximize their performance.

Since I started doing MACH 4 as a player, I am able to play more easily and effortlessly with a faster recovery time. I also will not allow anyone on my "team" again who does not have a positive approach to my game. Since I started doing MACH 4 as a coach, I emphasize what the player is doing well, not constantly reinforcing the word "mistake" to the player's mind because the mind will replicate what it is fed on a moment-to-moment or daily basis. Children often put their coaches on a higher pedestal than even their parents. When I am coaching, I want to be the best role model I can be. I know that what I say and do will either make or break a player's ability to become a stronger person and competitor. Is this not as important and necessary as teaching the physical skills needed to compete and win? MACH 4 teaches this and much more.

Too often today, the emphasis is put on who wins and who loses – as if the score was all that mattered. Dignity, integrity, and sportsmanship are often tossed aside in the quest for victory. Players, coaches, and parents often lose sight of why games are played. Everyone wants to win, and there is nothing wrong in that. But the extent to which people will go to win is alarming. We hear about parents and coaches who physically or emotionally abuse players whose ability or effort does not meet their expectations. None of this creates a healthy, winning environment.

For anyone who has enjoyed the thrill of athletic competition, there is no better feeling than walking off the court after a victory. The will to win is part of human nature (this is part of Darwin's survival of the fittest), but, unfortunately, the forces that prevent us from winning – negativity, sarcasm, domination – are also part of human nature. The next time you are near a tennis court, take a look around. Observe the behavior of the players, the coaches, the parents, and the fans. That behavior will tell you, regardless of the score, who is winning and who is losing. I believe in the power and effectiveness of positive mental training. This is the best way to coach so that your players can achieve the best results.

With this handbook, players, coaches, and parents will learn how to develop a prescription to win. If you are a coach or parent, you will learn effective strategies for creating a positive environment and getting the most out of your players and children. If you are a player, you will find effective ways to reach your maximum potential and put yourself in a position to win – and, at the same time, have fun and learn.

Development of the MACH 4® Mental Training System

My coach, Bev Raws, and I developed the MACH 4 Mental Training System as a result of my comeback to the women's professional tennis tour, beginning in January 2005. As Bev and I traveled to tournaments, it became more and more obvious to us the importance of the mental part of the game. When I first started back on the tour, we initially focused on making some changes in my movement. But we soon realized that my mindset before, during, and after my matches was more important than the technical part of the game.

I was being featured in my singles matches, and I had not played on the tour for 14 years! I was *very* nervous and had no confidence in my game. So, right before my match against Stephanie Dubois (ranked top 200 in the world) in Midland, Michigan, Bev said, "Just fake it." She told me to act confidently, whether I felt confident or not, and to pretend it did not bother me if I missed a shot. That was the beginning of the development of the MACH 4 System.

Bev has coached tennis for more than 25 years, so her expertise and approach to the game has helped me to be successful again on the tour. My new mental approach has helped me to improve more quickly and easily. I have incorporated the MACH 4 System into my current game and it has dramatically improved my performance. Although I was the "guinea pig" for this System, Bev and I have also used it with club-level, Division I, world-ranked juniors, and tour players with fast and positive results. We believe this System can help players at all levels improve, and that these concepts can also be applied to other sports and professions.

The only things a player can absolutely control and be responsible for are what he thinks, how he acts, and what he says to himself and others when he steps onto the court. How many coaches and players do you know who integrate into practice sessions these important components, which can help to maximize performance? Most coaches emphasize technique, but how many incorporate simple mental training tools to help coach their players' minds to win?

You do not have to be a psychologist to coach your players to become mentally stronger competitors; all you need are the tools. We believe that MACH 4 can help you become a better coach and your players become champions.

Principles of the MACH 4® Mental Training System

The MACH 4 Mental Training System consists of mental, body language, intensity level, and cueing language components. All of these are interrelated and work together to create a positive partnership with the mind and the body to ensure maximum performance. In order to achieve this, the mind and the body have to be trained to work together as a team.

I will now describe the principles of the MACH 4 System, and later I will describe each component and provide examples for clarification.

1. The System teaches that the mind controls the body. The mind tells the body what to do and, in tennis, for instance, what shot to hit. The body cannot always execute the shot, but the mind is always in charge.

2. The System is easy to incorporate during on-court practice sessions. Each time a player steps onto the court for practice, she can work on her mental toughness skills.

3. The System teaches how to have a consistent and solid performance during a match. When a player chooses to control his emotions and use his body language to project strength and confidence, he will play better

because he will be able to keep his best intensity level on every point.

4. The System can be individualized to a player's personality type. Because every player is different, what works for one player might not work for another. Our minds are as different as our bodies. The key is to figure out what cueing language produces the best results for each player.

5. The System enhances mental toughness, without the necessity, of having played for years. Even more than conditioning and shot production, my mental training is what allowed me to win a doubles pro tour title after 14 years of not playing competitively. By using the techniques in the MACH 4 System, I have been able to train more effectively in a shorter period of time, achieve success sooner rather than later, play with less effort and, more importantly, enjoy and appreciate the sport I love to play.

6. The physical recovery from a match is quicker using this System, as there is less "mind stress" during play. Stress causes muscles to tighten. Think of this formula:

   Negative Thoughts = Added Stress = Tight Muscles =

   Potential Injury = Non-Optimal Performance

   Why would any player risk using this type of performance formula in a match? What player would not want to play using less effort and be guaranteed that their performance would be enhanced?

7. The System teaches awareness. As Dr. Phil says, "You can't change what you don't acknowledge." By focusing on your mindset, you will begin to understand what changes you need to make in order to be successful.

Elements of the Mental Components of the MACH 4® Mental Training System

The mind controls the body and tells it what to do. The mental part of tennis involves how you think about your match before you walk on the court, what you say to yourself during the match, and what you choose to focus on during the match. Additional examples of the mental part of tennis are how you choose to carry yourself on the court, strategy and shot selection, how you choose to react to shots you miss, how you choose to react to what you think are bad line calls, maintaining your best intensity level, and what you and your coach choose to focus on after the match. The mental component of tennis – or any game that you play – is what you can say and do or think about to create the least amount of pressure on yourself so that you can perform at your best.

Here are some examples of different ways to approach the mental part of the game.

There Are No Mistakes – How many of you pay more attention to and expend more emotion on shots you miss rather than on shots you make? Too many players put a value judgment on their shots, particularly the ones they miss. By their reaction, you would sometimes think it was the end of the world when they miss a shot. The emotion that is attached to missing a shot reinforces the miss and causes the player to hold onto the miss longer than is necessary. If you respond to a miss and not to those you hit well, you are reinforcing the negative instead of the positive; your mind will recreate the shots that you attached the most feeling to during the match. It is important to remember that there are no mistakes; you either make it or you miss it. Next time you miss, try saying to yourself, *No problem. I'll make the next one.* Next time you hit a winning shot, get excited and say to yourself, *Great shot. Way to go!*

No Free Points – How many of you give away free points to your opponents? Most players, of course, will not admit to doing this! But if they think about it, they would have to admit that they do give away free points. A free point is the point after you miss an "easy" shot. Bev and I developed the "no free points" concept after a match I played in Pelham, Alabama, against an 18-year-old from Russia. I lost 7–5 in the third set. I played a very good match, but as I was talking to Bev afterward about some of the easy shots I missed, she said, "There are no easy shots. Stop attaching a judgment to them." She also noticed that after I missed what looked like a simple shot, I would lose the next two or three points. So we decided to experiment with stopping the run of "free points" I was giving my opponent. Now, whenever I miss a shot in a match, I try to win the next point no matter what – or at least make my opponent *earn* the next point. If I am serving, I get my first serve in. If I am returning, I get my return in. This change in focus from reacting to the miss to focusing on winning the next point helped take my mind off the miss and focus on the point at hand. I took this as a challenge because I do not ever want to give my opponent a run of free or unearned points. Bev and I could detect a difference in my level of play in my next match. I made a conscious effort to not put any negative emotion into my misses. Remember, the missed shot is not the free point. It is the point after the miss that is a potential free point.

Antidotes – Most players only think about their *own* game and what they are doing right or wrong. When players do this, they are missing out on another important dimension of match play: what they can do to make their opponent "stand down." So, instead of only focusing on your own game, ask yourself the following questions about your opponent: What types of shots does she not like to hit? What are her weaknesses? What can I do to throw her off her game or get her out of her rhythm?

Eliminate Anger – At the height of my tennis career in the 1980s, I would often get angry in my singles matches. Whether it happened because of disputed line calls, my opponent's behavior, or missed shots, anger never helped me win. Anger interrupts concentration and takes away energy needed to play at the best intensity. Reactive emotions, like anger, become habits. Habits can be changed with awareness and practice. Instead of getting angry, stop and say to yourself, *Come on, it's only one point; win the next one.* Create situations in practice such as bad line calls to teach your players how to remain calm. Remaining calm and focused ensures an easier way to win.

Self-Talk – Tennis players at times say the most destructive things to themselves on the court. There seems to be a constant negative dialogue going on, particularly after the player misses what they perceive to be an easy shot. You know the type of player. They are the ones who say (very loudly, much of the time), "I can't believe I missed that shot. It was so easy." This is usually just a cover-up for a lack of confidence. Next time your opponent starts talking to herself in this manner, she is telegraphing to you that she is not confident in her abilities. Do you do the same thing? Why give an opponent any opportunity to see how you might be feeling? Next time you miss a shot you think you should not have missed, encourage yourself and act like the miss was no big deal. Opponents do NOT like to see a player who looks confident and strong the entire match. It is unnerving. Try this approach and you will be amazed at the results.

Shot Selection – Many players do not think that shot selection is a mental skill that must be practiced. Since the mind tells the body where to hit the shot, it is critical for a player to monitor and test these choices before the actual match. The player (her body) cannot always execute the shot, but where she chooses to hit the ball is a mental process – for example, when a player chooses to go for a down-the-line shot on a ball that should be hit crosscourt, or when a player tries to drop shot from the baseline on set point. These are examples of misses that can be avoided with the proper mental training. One way to work on shot selection is to play high-percentage tennis rather than going for an outright winner when you are out of position or going for an ace on match point. Instead, train your mind and body to play high-percentage tennis.

Strategy – Strategy is also a mental process. Again, a player cannot always execute the shot or strategy, but he can scout an opponent, determine how to play against a certain opponent, and stick with his game plan. These are all mental skills that can be learned with awareness and practice.

Defining Moments – There are certain points in a match that determine whether a player is going to win or lose. Matches come down to these defining moments. I have played with doubles partners who have taken me to the brink of winning, only to double fault or choose to hit a low-percentage shot or decide to get angry. Can a player make her first serve? Make the return? Choose the appropriate shot when it counts? These moments define a player. Train yourself to play high-percentage tennis when the game, set, or match is on the line. Resist the temptation to win the match in a blaze of glory by going for an ace or trying to hit an outright winner on the return. Champions play high-percentage tennis during defining moments.

Focus, Focus, Focus - How many times have you said that to your players? Some players have difficulty concentrating. Telling players to focus when the ball is in play is a great start to help them not to feel so overwhelmed about having to concentrate for an entire match. The following example is a way to dialogue with your player so that he can look at it a different way that seems easier. Tell your player to focus *just* when the ball is in play (only about 5–15 seconds at a time). If you break it down, a complete tennis match only lasts about 20–25 minutes. The rest of the match is spent picking up balls and taking drinks of water. Most players can commit to stay focused for 20–25 minutes!

Be a Good Partner – to Yourself, Your Doubles Partner and Your Teammates – Being a good partner to yourself means paying attention to your self-talk, limiting and eventually stopping negative self-talk, and encouraging yourself. Being a good partner in doubles means being careful about the manner and tone of how you speak to your partner, not acting like you are in charge on the court, making the match a team effort, and encouraging your partner. Train your mind to be a good partner.

Body Language Components of the MACH 4® Mental Training System

Body language will energize a player. From the moment you arrive at the tennis tournament or competition, your body language, how you carry yourself, is paramount. Do you project a confident, fighter image? Do you walk with a spring in your step, your head held high, and your shoulders back? How do you walk onto the court? You can use body language not only to intimidate your opponent before the competition even begins but to keep your own nerves at bay. That is the magic of MACH 4 – no matter who the opponent is or how they are performing, you can project confidence with your own actions so that energy/ intensity levels will remain strong and concentrated rather than being wasted or given away to the opponent. It is easy to do, and it is a choice. Try this experiment: sit in a chair, put your hands in your lap, drop your shoulders and look down. You will feel your energy drop too. Now, sit up tall with your shoulders back, head up, and look straight ahead. Can you feel the energy center in your chest just by making this simple adjustment?

During competition, it is critical to display powerful body language every moment of the match. For example, how you walk in between points, how you sit during the changeover, how you react to a missed shot, how you react to a well played point, and how you react to a winning shot. Your body language should stay strong and confident no matter what is happening on the court. How many times during a match will a player allow his energy/intensity to drop after not executing a shot? How long will it take to restore the energy/intensity so that "free points" to the opponent are minimized and concentration is not disrupted? Why take the chance? If body language will easily help an athlete to be able to sustain positive emotions and energy and concentration, then why not practice it and use it to win?

In developing the body language components of the MACH 4 System, Bev and I borrowed some terms and concepts from the martial arts. The same types of philosophies that students use in tae kwon do or karate can be applied to tennis and all other sports. Use these seven body language components to immediately improve your performance.

Stance – Send a message of strength. The way a player stands to serve or stands to receive serve or stands at the net can have an impact on an opponent. Do you stand in a confident and intimidating manner before you serve? Does your service return stance project confidence and strength? Do you stand at the net looking like you want to volley? If you can answer yes to all of these questions, then you are on your way to causing your opponent to miss at that important moment when she contacts the ball.

Eyes – Use your eyes to make your opponent stand down. Your eyes can be a very powerful source of energy. Bev and I are friends with Duc Huy Dang, a grand master in tae kwon do who has a martial arts academy in Westminster, California. Bev asked him to show her how the eyes are used in the martial arts. He demonstrated "the look" and she literally felt an energy push her back. Projecting confidence with your eyes says, "I own you" no matter what is happening in the match.

Act Confident (or just fake it) – Most players do not think about it, but acting confident is so important. Would you rather play against someone who walks around the court confidently and in control? Or someone who throws her racquet and shares a constant, negative dialogue about how badly she is playing? It is much more difficult to play against someone who projects calmness and confidence. During a match, confidence can come and go, so whenever you are not feeling it, fake it – act as if you are confident. This will help keep your shots strong and prevent your opponent from knowing how you feel.

Emotion – Emotions such as anger and fear shut down a player's ability to use intuition during a match. When negative emotions are dominating a player's mind, intuition, a *gut feeling,* cannot occur. When a player stays calm, determined, and focused, she will be able to allow her mind to access her "sixth sense" which is valuable during competition. Imagine being able to *know* ahead of time where your opponent is going to direct the ball. As Billie Jean King said, "I played with my head, my heart, and my *gut*". We coach our players to play with emotions that help them to win. Emotions that help athletes to win are: passion, joy, and excitement. Other important factors include saying *YES* after executing a winning shot, determination, and competitiveness. Emotions that cause athletes to lose are anger, fear, disappointment, and frustration. Other losing factors are crying (on the court) and whining.

Ask your players which list of emotions they want to pick from – those that help them to win or those that cause them to lose. All champions will pick from the list of emotions that help them to win. Train your emotions to help you play better by practicing with focus, passion, and determination. Eliminate anger, fear, disappointment, frustration, and whining by replacing them with emotions and actions that help you to win. You cannot be joyful and whining at the same time. You cannot be smiling and crying at the same time. Most importantly, positive emotions will allow you to access your intuition which will make it much easier for you to win.

Breathing – Use your breathing to bring in energy. Breathing is related to heart rate. It is very important to keep your heart rate within a certain range in order to play the next point with your best intensity. Both the mind and body will stay more connected when the heart rate is not too high. That is why it is so important to take your allotted 20 seconds between points – to bring your heart rate down. A player has a certain amount of energy reserve. We tell the players we coach that as they breathe in, they are bringing energy into their bodies. This way the player is thinking she is always filling her energy reserve.

Another aspect of breathing is when a player makes a sound when she hits the ball. We encourage our players to make a sound when they hit the ball to ensure they are not holding their breath. It also helps some players enhance their concentration. However, we do not endorse making too much of a sound as it gives away too much energy to the opponent. Perhaps if Maria Sharapova realized how much energy she is wasting by grunting so loudly, she might choose not to do it.

Stand Down – Take your opponent out of her best game. What can you do to get your opponent to "stand down" – to get her out of her comfort zone on the court? Again, most players think only about themselves or their missed shots or opportunities rather than playing certain shots to throw off their opponent. You can also get your opponent to stand down by the look in your eyes and how you stand to serve or receive serve, as well as how you carry yourself on and off the court. Matches can be won before the first point is even played because of how a player perceives her opponent.

Rituals – Use rituals that help you feel mentally and physically stronger. There are things a player can do to help himself relax and get in a rhythm. Lleyton Hewitt tugs at his shorts, touches his cap, and stares down his opponent. Tracy Austin used to fiddle with her necklaces right before she returned serve. Rituals can help calm an athlete and put him in a comfort zone for optimal performance. Discover your own rituals and use them to play better.

Intensity Level Component of the MACH 4® Mental Training System

It is so important to recognize physical responses to match moments. Intensity level has to do with not only a physical feeling but also with footwork and how hard a player swings at the ball. A drop in intensity of just 10% will affect results. For example, if a player is serving for the match and her intensity level decreases, it is very likely that she will not perform her best that game. Most tennis players have a tendency to slow down their hand on the serve at important times during matches. This is a decrease in intensity. When a player slows her hand down on her serve, the pace of her serve decreases and this gives the opponent the opportunity to hit a better return. It is possible to have too high of an intensity level as well. What if a player swings too hard at the serve, causing the ball to sail long?

In the MACH 4 System, we rate intensity level on a scale from 1–5. In this System, 1–2 = low intensity, 3–4 = medium intensity, and 5 = high intensity. When a player is swinging at the ball with her intensity level at 1 or 2, she will not win many points. When a player is swinging at the ball with her intensity level at 5, she will either be exhausted by the third or fourth game of the match, or she will be missing so many shots that she will lose quickly. We coach our players to swing at the ball with a 3 or 4 intensity level, and only on some shots with a

5 intensity level. We do not recommend using a 5 intensity level on match point! Remember to individualize this to your player's style and technique. A level 4 on one player's serve will be different than a level 4 on another player's serve.

This focus on intensity level has literally helped the players we coach improve overnight. This fast improvement is a result of the focus on a physical feeling. Intensity relates to some physical movement or feeling in the body. Slowing the hand down on ground strokes or serves can be felt by the player and then changed immediately. It is easier to feel intensity than think about technique, particularly during a match. The mind cannot be bombarded with thinking about technique during matches. Whatever technique a player has going into a match is what will be used. We have seen by our players' performance that when their minds focus on intensity levels, it stops emotions such as fear and anger from derailing their momentum. Our players tell us they are no longer afraid to go for their shots. They play high-percentage tennis, and they are more willing to try new concepts and strategy and add more shots to their game.

What I am mindful of when I play is keeping my intensity level in the 3–4 range. This takes awareness and practice. I had no idea that I was slowing my hand down on my serve at certain times during a match. Bev noticed it and brought it to my attention. This helped create more awareness for me. You cannot change what you are not aware of in your game. So, determine what your best intensity level is, monitor it during practice, and then make it a priority to maintain your best intensity level during practices and matches. Best intensity will create optimal results.

Best intensity = Best performance

Cueing Language Components of the MACH 4® Mental Training System

Cueing is a term that has been used in the aerobics industry. Bev and I have found cueing to be helpful not only with my own tennis, but with players we teach at all levels of the game. It also adds humor to practices. When players are less intense, their muscles remain more relaxed which helps them execute their shots.

Cues are words or phrases that can trigger certain mental, emotional, visual, and physical responses. Cueing can and should also be individualized. A cue that works for one player might not work for another. It is important for coaches and players to come up with cues that are meaningful for them.

Martina Navratilova loved the cueing I used with her when I coached her during the 2005 WTT Boston Lobsters season. Hey, if it is good enough for Martina, it is good enough for the rest of us!

Bev and I have coined certain terms and phrases that are descriptive of specific shots and situations. We first teach the technique involved in the shot. Then, when the player understands the physical way to hit the shot, we only need to cue them with a word or phrase. It really helps to keep things simple and fun.

Meatball – This is one of the most difficult shots in the game. The meatball is that high, slow ball that you volley. It is a high ball with no pace on it, and it usually happens on the third shot in doubles. The player either hits it in the back fence or the bottom of the net. Usually players will say, "I can't believe I missed that shot. It was so easy." Most players do not give the meatball enough attention, precisely because they think it is so easy. The keys to hitting the meatball are to move to the ball with your feet first (rather than standing and taking a big swing), keep your chin up and look at the ball, and have a short follow-through.

Chunky Monkey – I love the Ben and Jerry's ice cream flavor called Chunky Monkey so much that I named this shot after it. The chunky monkey is the shot you can hit when an opponent has pulled you off the court and you need time to recover. Or it is the shot you can hit when your opponent likes to hit low, hard balls with lots of pace. The chunky monkey is an off-pace ball that has some topspin on it. It bounces about two or three feet from your opponent's baseline. It is a relatively high bouncing ball that pushes your opponent back. I can sometimes hit it so that it goes over my opponent's head or, even better, over the fence! Martina's 'slender monkey' shot is a lower bouncing version.

Bop – Bev coined this shot. The bop is a shot you can use to defend against the lob. This is a really useful shot for club players, but I have even used the bop on the tour. The bop is used in lieu of hitting an overhead or taking a chance at injury by turning and chasing a lob. It also allows you to maintain control of the net. When your opponent lobs, move back underneath the ball, extend your arm up toward the ball, and, once you make contact, stop your swing – do not break your wrist (like on an overhead) or follow-through, then move back to net. Too many players try to hit an overhead when they are off-balance or clearly out of position to do so. The bop is a great shot to have in your repertoire.

First Strike – Martina loved this phrase, and it helped her win a pivotal match for the Boston Lobsters against the New York Sportimes that put us into the playoffs. Martina was playing against Jenny Hopkins, a very good player ranked in the top 150 in the world. Jenny was running Martina all over the court. I knew it was in Martina's best interest to end the points as quickly as possible, rather than getting into long rallies. One of Martina's best combos is when she returns serve and comes in behind it to volley. So I told her to do first strike. She said, "What's first strike?" I quickly told her to get "Jenny running before she gets you running. Take the first ball you get and make an aggressive shot. Hit this next return down the line and come into the net." Martina caught on quickly (she is, of course, very smart!) and she ended up beating Jenny.

Lock & Load – Bev swears that David Kelley, producer of *Boston Legal* and many other shows, "stole" this line from her. She was using it before the show even came out! Lock & load is used to get a player to stand in a strong position, with her arms out in front, ready to hit the ball, usually on a volley. Lots of players allow their arms to collapse when they are at the net, and they are not ready to hit the ball. This cue also works well with the initial turn on the ground strokes.

The Closer – Players on the tour seem to have the most difficulty with this shot. It is the mid-court ball that usually comes a bit slower and higher. If hit correctly, the closer can either be an outright winner or cause your opponent to hit a weak enough shot so that you can then put it away. The most common response to this ball is to over-hit it or to hit it too close to the line. Remember, it is not always about how hard you hit the ball, but where you place it.

Land It – This is one of my favorites. I say this to myself on game points when I am serving. The tendency is to "press" on your first serve when you have an ad point. So my thought is to hit a good first serve that causes my opponent to hit a weak reply. I want to land it. There is nothing better than hitting a good first serve on game point rather than going for an ace and missing, or double faulting.

Leave it On the Court - This is also something I say to myself on the court. I want to make sure that I have given my best effort and that I have not short-changed myself in any way. I want to be able to say that I did the best I could on that day. I do not want to come off the court second-guessing myself or saying I should have done this or that. I want to come off knowing I did everything I could to win. I want to leave it on the court.

Points – When I first started my comeback, I thought I would be able to win some matches right away, but I found out that was not going to happen. I had been out of the game for 14 years, and there is no substitute for match play. So I went from focusing on winning matches to focusing on winning points. This change in focus helped me because it started to bring up thoughts and feelings from when I was on the tour in the early 1980s. It made me realize that everything I had back then to make me a champion was still inside of me. I just needed to give it time to come out. There are no short cuts. Eventually, I started winning points, then games, then sets, then matches, and then a tournament. Focus on one point at a time.

20/1 – Each shot I execute is worth 20 points; those missed, only one point. I reinforce to myself what I do well, not what I miss. I do not need my mind working against me in a match. The body and the mind are a team that must be good partners to one another at all times. This 20/1 will especially help those players who want to stop judging their misses. That is really just a waste of time.

Aim for the Service Line – This has worked well for elite junior players and tour players who like to hit swinging volleys from mid-court. One thing Bev and I noticed when tour players were taking the ball out of the air at mid-court was that they would usually hit the ball long. Bev started saying, "Aim for the service line." This quickly cured missing the swinging volley long.

Spike – Besides being the name of my parents' cat, this is the shot you hit when you get a high ball close to the net. It can be an antidote to the meatball!

Implementation of the MACH 4® Mental Training System

What is the most effective way for a coach (or parent) to use the MACH 4 Mental Training System? Start with yourself. Be aware of your own self-talk, body language, intensity level, and manner of speaking with your athletes.

Coaches that are negative and critical and feel that they must yell at their players to help them perform are not creating strong, confident athletes. Athletes who have been coached like this will, more often than not, not come through at a big moment when they must perform. Coaches who use this style of communicating run the risk that their players will create negative results because they are more comfortable with negative feedback.

Coaches who are caring and have their athlete's best interest at heart will always create winning results. Their players become better people as well as stronger competitors. Players who are asked to focus more on what they executed well in competition, as opposed to what shots they missed, will create more opportunities to win... not lose.

Many coaches forget that it is not about them venting their own personal feelings or frustrations in practices or competition. Everyone wants so much for their players to win. It is up to all coaches to understand that being harsh or angry will never produce truly positive results.

What is your style of coaching? Do you empower your players to win or do you give their minds more thoughts that cause them to lose? Ask yourself, do my players have fun and love what they are doing? Do they want to win for themselves and me? If the answers are yes, then as a coach, you have not only done a great job, you have given your players the ultimate chance to win in sports and life.

The Importance of MACH 4 in Practice

How many hours each week do you spend playing/coaching in practice? How many hours each week do you spend playing/coaching matches? All athletes and coaches spend much more time in practice than in competition. Just think about Olympic athletes. They practice for years, then all of their training and preparation can come down to just one performance. But the rest of us are able to practice and then test our skills regularly in competitions. Football players practice five or six days a week and play one game a week. Baseball and basketball players practice several days a week and play games several days a week. Tennis players practice for weeks or months and then play several tournaments in a row. My point is that athletes spend the majority of their time practicing. So why not incorporate mental training into practice?

Examples of MACH 4 in Practice

Bev and I are coaching tour players and aspiring tour players in the Phoenix area. We have incorporated the MACH 4 System into all of the practice sessions. When we initially began coaching these players, they believed that doing drills and training physically was much more important than mental training. So at one of the first meetings I asked them how much of tennis is mental. They agreed that it was at least 90%. I then asked them if they spend 90% of their time on the mental part of the game. No, of course not. After only working with them for three weeks on MACH 4, the players are convinced of the importance of the mental part of the game. They all believe that MACH 4 has helped them tremendously.

Bev and I believe that intensity level is critical in tennis – or any sport for that matter – because it is related to a physical feeling. We constantly monitor the players' intensity level in practice. On certain days when they do baseline drills on a ball machine, they will hit a series of eight balls in a row at a target. If I feel like a player's intensity level is too low, I will ask her what number on a scale from 1–5 she would say her intensity level was that series. By doing this, I am trying to raise her awareness so that she can begin to independently monitor her own intensity level.

It is very important to involve your players and ask them questions rather than always telling them what to do. Our goal is to raise awareness and self sufficiency. That is why MACH 4 is so valuable. Coaches can easily use it during practice. They can give their players immediate feedback; research shows that feedback is most effective when given right away.

We also monitor how the players react to certain situations during practice, especially when they miss. We specifically look at their body language and listen to what they say. At the beginning, we are constantly speaking with the players about their body language and verbalizations. But after only a short period of time, we rarely have to talk with them about negative body language and dialogue. I think what turned it around was our philosophy of "there are no mistakes." We would frequently ask them why they gave so much more emotion, attention, and focus to their missed shots instead of to the shots they executed. When the players changed their perception about missing, they played with less fear.

Another technique we use during the ball machine drill is to ask the players to act as if they are playing a point. Instead of mindlessly hitting eight balls in a row at a target, we ask them to hit the ball as if they are playing a point in a match. We want them to hit the ball with the intensity they would in a tournament. The players love when we do this. They gain more awareness regarding their shots, and their concentration level increases.

During the ball machine drills, I also like to ask the players what cues they use to help them make technique corrections. During a series of eight balls, if a player is reacting to hitting a couple of balls into the net, I will ask her what she is saying to herself to change that shot. At first the players did not have answers to my questions because they were too busy getting angry or slumping around the court. This is a great way to incorporate mental training with technique because it teaches the players constructive ways to deal with their misses. Using cues helps to eliminate emotional reactions associated with misses. The focus shifts from emotionally judging missed shots which disrupts concentration to positive cueing that improves performance.

Another example of how we use MACH 4 in practice is shown during practice when the players are serving at targets. Instead of just acting like they are hitting balls at targets, we ask them to practice as if they are serving in a match. We want them to practice what they will think, the rituals they will use, the physical feelings and emotions associated with serving in a match, and the best intensity level they will use on their first serve. For example, we might ask them to pretend like they are serving the first point in a match. Then we might call out certain scenarios, such as: you are serving at match point in the Wimbledon final. It makes it fun and it also generates match-like thoughts, feelings, and emotions rather than "this is just practice."

During scheduled practice matches, we remind the players to be mindful of what they are doing during the 20 seconds between points and on the change over. Does their body language and self-talk help them to stay strong and win? Our players now know how important each moment of a match is and what actions and words help them to maximize their performance.

MACH 4®
Mental Training System Worksheets & Questionnaire

Several worksheets have been created to help players and coaches implement the MACH 4 Mental Training System and track results. I will briefly describe each one and how to complete them. The worksheets are at the end of the Handbook.

MACH 4® Mental Training System Goals Worksheet

Before your season begins or when you begin coaching a new player, one of the first things you want to do is to complete the Goals Worksheet. Observe your new players for about a week and then meet with them individually. It is important to have an observation period in order to watch them practice and to get to know them so that you can help them fill out the Goals Worksheet. During these meetings, we discuss their emotional, body language, and intensity goals and what cues they will use to reach these goals. This is a good time to brainstorm with your players and help them discover what will work for them. This is also how to individualize MACH 4 to a player's personality type, since what works for one player might not work for another. Also, it will probably take some time for you and your player to figure out what her best intensity level is and what it feels like. The intensity questions at the bottom of the page may be broken down even further if you think it will help your players. For example, ground strokes can be divided into forehand and backhand. Some players have a different intensity level on their forehand than they do on their backhand. Again, individualize this to your player. This document is a work in progress for the players, because as they become more aware, they will come up with different cues from time to time. Once the worksheet is completed, you will be able to help your players implement their emotional, body language, and intensity goals during practice.

MACH 4® Mental Training System Daily Point Worksheet

We have created a daily point and bonus point system using MACH 4 components of body language and intensity. Coaches can rate their players each day regarding their body language and intensity during tennis drills, footwork and conditioning drills, weight training and exercises, and practice matches. This point system has been effective with players that we coach because they are so competitive. We stress to them that we are doing this to help make them not only become champions but better people and that we do not want them to see this as a competition with each other.

We also have MACH 4 group meetings with the players several times a week. MACH 4 has become more than just a mental training system for on the court. We also use it to train certain off-court behaviors, or actions, as well. We have created a bonus point system incorporating MACH 4 with off-court behaviors such as saying "please" and "thank you," picking up after themselves, being kind to one another, following rules, picking up balls without being asked, following their nutrition plan, etc. We have encouraged them to think of each other as being on the same team. They now contribute ideas to make the team stronger.

MACH 4 has quickly improved their behavior, raised their self-esteem, and elevated their level of play. The best testimony is from the players. They play with less fear and better results. When we ask them why their games are so much stronger, they all say "MACH 4."

MACH 4® Mental Training System Match Intensity Worksheet

This worksheet is designed for the coach to chart a player's intensity level during match play on a scale from 1 to 5. The coach will be able to chart the player's intensity level on the first and second serve and return of serve. There is also a space on the right side of the worksheet to chart the intensity level of the last shot hit on each point. For example, what intensity level does your player have if the last shot of the rally is a passing shot? Does her intensity level decrease on the passing shot? In other words, does she slow her hand down and not swing as hard when she has to come up with a passing shot on game point?

This worksheet can be used for a complete match or the coach may choose to only chart certain games. For example, the coach may want to chart his player's first service game and first return game. Then he may want to wait until a later time in the first set. For example, a good time to chart your player's intensity level is when she is serving for the first set. During a recent practice match, one of our players was serving for the first set at 5–4. At 5–4 30–0, she decided to slow her hand down on her serve to about a 2 or 3 intensity level to just "try and get it in." Needless to say, her opponent broke her serve and they ended up playing a tie-break for the set. Now, when she plays, she uses cues such as "Do the first serve", "ball toss", and "concentrate".

When we discuss intensity level with our players, we consistently highlight the advantages of keeping their ground stroke intensity level within the 3-4 range. One important advantage is a player uses less energy in the rallies during the match which allows him to maintain his serve at a 4 – 5 intensity level. By determining each player's best intensity level, the results are weaker returns from his opponent, points are ended more quickly, which leads to shorter matches, less chance of injury, and more energy for his next match.

MACH 4® Mental Training System Post-Match Intensity Worksheet

This worksheet is completed by the player after her match. The player rates her perceived average intensity level for each set on a scale from 1 to 5. Some areas that are covered on this worksheet include warm-up, footwork, ground strokes, and return of serve. Once your player has rated herself, go over the form with her to see how accurately she perceived her intensity level. This is important because you can determine how well she is able to judge her own intensity level. If she is way off the mark, this is an opportunity for you to teach her how to physically feel the difference between intensity levels. Again, this helps create awareness so that meaningful changes can be made.

MACH 4® Mental Training System Free Points & Cueing Worksheet

This worksheet is completed by the coach during the player's match. When we first talked with our players about free points, we would only chart how many free points they gave away during their practice matches. There is also a space for observed cues your player does during a match like looking at her strings between points or slapping herself on the thigh after executing a shot. This worksheet is for very specific skills and can be combined with the Match Intensity Worksheet.

MACH 4® Mental Training System Tennis Questionnaire

I have developed a questionnaire that our players fill out after every practice match or tournament match. It has concepts associated with MACH 4. For example, some of the statements are: I used cues to help me play well; I acted like a champion; and I played at my best intensity level.

Conclusion

MACH 4 positively impacts behaviors both on and off the court. It is more than just about tennis or competition; it makes a difference in people's lives. MACH 4 helps people become better people. It helps build respect, increase emotional control, improve communication, increase self-discipline, and create better relationships.

The best endorsements for the benefits of MACH 4 are from the players. Some of the players we have worked with have this to say about what MACH 4 has done for them:

"MACH 4 helps me control my emotions."

"MACH 4 has helped me in my life.... I am now nicer to the people who are around me."

"MACH 4 helps me to understand my temperament and to control my emotions better on the court."

"MACH 4 has helped me be a stronger player.... it has also helped me be a good person with others."

"MACH 4 even helps me off the court."

"MACH 4 taught me how to focus and get my intensity back." "MACH 4 has taught me many things... how to help myself and how to become mentally and physically strong.... right now, I am recovering from an injury and MACH 4 has really helped me with that."

"With MACH 4 everything has gotten better on and off the court."

"Using MACH 4, I don't waste my energy and I do not feel as tired after my matches as I did before.... Now I have such a feeling that nobody can beat me."

"Mach 4 really helped us a lot, especially in doubles. We were like one team. Our intensity during the whole match was about 4 so that's why we were winning our matches easily. We won all these doubles because of Oksana. She played great. She served big serves and I played volleys. If she didn't I don't think the result would be so high. We weren't arguing at each other after misses, we just said "Come on, it's okay, don't worry, do the next point". This way we didn't give any free points. But sometimes when Oksana's energy and intensity were dropping down I came to her and reminded her about it and she listened to me. Almost all girls were impressed with our doubles. They said: "Oh, you are such a strong doubles team. We like your game" or "It's good that you're always playing doubles together!" Now we know how and when to raise our intensity and energy, I always said some cues, especially before my serve. I tried to play percentage tennis "not too soon down the line". Before Mach 4 I was very tired after the match, but now I know how not to waste my energy during the tournament. The line calls were very bad! But we tried not to pay attention to it. We played calm and concentrated."

The MACH 4 Mental Training System can be used in any sport. I have focused on tennis, but the same philosophy and concepts can be applied to football, baseball, basketball, golf, swimming, or any other sport that you play or coach. Athletic competition often comes down to moments. MACH 4 connects the physical conditioning and technique with the mind to maximize an athlete's performance. MACH 4 gives your player or child the mental edge to win.

MACH 4®
Mental Training System
Goals Worksheet

Date: ____________________

Emotional goals for the next month.
(What emotions make it hard for me to win?)

1. ______________________________________

2. ______________________________________

3. ______________________________________

What cues will I use to achieve my emotional goals?
(What will I say to myself?)

1. ______________________________________

2. ______________________________________

3. ______________________________________

Body language goals for the next month.
(What do I want to look like on the court?)

1. ______________________________________

2. ______________________________

3. ______________________________

What cues will I use to achieve my body language goals?

1. ______________________________

2. ______________________________

3. ______________________________

Rate the following on a scale from 1 to 5:

What is my best intensity level on my groundstrokes?

____

What is my best intensity level on my first serve?

____

What is my best intensity level on my second serve?

____

What is my best intensity level on my footwork?

____

MACH 4®
Mental Training System
Daily Point Worksheet

Rate 1 (low) to 5 (high)

BL = Body Language INT = Intensity ACT = Actions NTR = Nutrition

Month ______________

	Strength & Conditioning				Tennis				Off Court			+/-	Daily Total
	Footwork/ Conditioning		Flexibility Rehab Core Circuit		Drills		Match Play						
	BL	INT	BL	INT	BL	INT	BL	INT	BL	NTR	ACT		
1													
2													
3													
4													
5													
6													
7													
8													
9													
10													
11													
12													
13													
14													
15													
16													
17													
18													
19													
20													

21													
22													
23													
24													
25													
26													
27													
28													
29													
30													
31													

MACH 4®
Mental Training System
Match Intensity Worksheet

DATE______________ PLAYER________________

OPPONENT_________ COACH ________________

WINNER___________ FINAL SCORE ___________

Rate the player's intensity level on serve and/or return of serve using the following scale:

1-2 = low intensity (LI) 3-4 = medium intensity (MI)
5 = high intensity (HI)

In the space to the right, rate the player's intensity level on the last shot of the point using the following system:

Forehand = FH	Backhand = BH
High Forehand = HFH	Low Forehand = LFH
High Backhand = HBH	Low Backhand = LBH
Volley = FHV; BHV	Swinging Volley = SV
Overhead = OH	Approach shot = APS

Passing shot = PS
Winner = W
Crosscourt = CC
Return of serve = RS
Double Fault = DF

Short ball = SB
Ace = A
Down the line = DL
Drop shot = DS
Lob = Lob

Set Score_______ Server _____ OR Receiver _______

Game Score _______1ST ___ 2ND ___ __________

_______1ST ___ 2ND ___ __________

_______1ST ___ 2ND ___ __________

_______1ST ___ 2ND ___ __________

_______1ST ___ 2ND ___ __________

_______1ST ___ 2ND ___ __________

_______1ST ___ 2ND ___ __________

_______1ST ___ 2ND ___ __________

_______1ST ___ 2ND ___ __________

_______1ST ___ 2ND ___ __________

_______1ST ___ 2ND ___ __________

_______1ST ___ 2ND ___ __________

_______1ST ___ 2ND ___ __________

_______ 1ST ___ 2ND ___ __________

_______ 1ST ___ 2ND ___ __________

_______ 1ST ___ 2ND ___ __________

_______ 1ST ___ 2ND ___ __________

_______ 1ST ___ 2ND ___ __________

MACH 4®
Mental Training System
Post-Match Intensity Worksheet

Player: ________________ Date: ________________

Rate your average intensity level for each set using the following scale:

1-2 = low intensity (LI) 3-4 = medium intensity (MI)
5 = high intensity (HI)

	1st Set	2nd Set	3rd Set
walking	_______	_______	_______
warm-up	_______	_______	_______
footwork	_______	_______	_______
groundstrokes	_______	_______	_______
approach shots	_______	_______	_______
volleys	_______	_______	_______
overheads	_______	_______	_______
passing shots	_______	_______	_______

return of 1st serve	_______	_______	_______
return of 2nd serve	_______	_______	_______
1st serve	_______	_______	_______
2nd serve	_______	_______	_______

Match Score: ____

Match comments with Coach:

____

____

____

____

MACH 4®
Mental Training System
Free Points & Cueing Worksheet

DATE________________ PLAYER__________________

OPPONENT__________ COACH _________________

WINNER_____________ SCORE __________________

Free Points : Set Score_________ Game Score ________

Free Points: Set Score _________ Game Score ________

Free Points : Set Score_________ Game Score ________

Free Points: Set Score _________ Game Score ________

Observed Cues ___________________________________

Observed Cues ___________________________________

Observations of opponent's comments and body language:

____

____

____

____

____

MACH 4®
Mental Training System
Tennis Questionnaire

1. I played at my best intensity level.

   (a.) not at all (b.) sometimes
   (c.) most of the time (d.) all of the time

2. I was a good partner to myself (and my doubles partner).

   (a) not at all (b) sometimes
   (c) most of the time (d) all of the time

3. I acted calm and confident.

   (a) not at all (b) sometimes
   (c) most of the time (d) all of the time

4. I used my emotions to help myself play better.

   (a) not at all (b) sometimes
   (c) most of the time (d) all of the time

5. The words I said to myself helped me play stronger.

   (a) not at all (b) sometimes
   (c) most of the time (d) all of the time

6. I acted like a Champion.

(a) not at all (b) sometimes
(c) most of the time (d) all of the time

7. I kept thinking about the shots I missed.

(a) not at all (b) sometimes
(c) most of the time (d) all of the time

8. I gave away free points.

(a) not at all (b) sometimes
(c) most of the time (d) all of the time

9. I focused when the ball was in play.

(a) not at all (b) sometimes
(c) most of the time (d) all of the time

10. I used cues to help myself play well.

(a) not at all (b) sometimes
(c) most of the time (d) all of the time

11. I did everything to help myself and not my opponent.

(a) not at all (b) sometimes
(c) most of the time (d) all of the time

About the Author

Anne Smith, Ph.D., won her place in the history books of all-time winners with 10 Grand Slam championships in doubles and mixed doubles from 1980 to 1984. She is one of only 20 women in the Open Era of tennis who have won 10 or more Grand Slam titles. She has won three US Open titles, two Wimbledon titles, four French Open titles and one Australian Open title. She has been a member of the Wightman Cup and Federation Cup teams. She was ranked No. 1 in the world in doubles in 1980 and 1981 and reached a career-high No.12 in the world in singles in 1982. Anne was a member of three World TeamTennis Championship Teams – the Boston Lobsters, the San Antonio Racquets, and the Dallas Stars. She went on to win the 35-and-over women's doubles at the U.S. Open and Wimbledon in 1997.

As a junior, Anne was No. 1 in Texas from the 12s through the 18s. When she was 15, she was No. 1 in Texas in both 16 and 18 singles. At age 17, Anne went to Paris and became the first American to win the French Open Junior Singles Championship. She holds 21 national junior and adult titles. In Texas, Anne was awarded the coveted Mary Lowden Award for sportsmanship four years in a row from 1974-1977. She also received the Maureen Connolly Brinker award in 1977 for the most outstanding full season performance in the 18-and-under division in the U.S. Anne was born and raised in Dallas, Texas and has been inducted into the Texas Tennis Hall of Fame.

After her active tennis career, Anne returned to Trinity University and earned her Bachelor's degree. She then enrolled at the University of Texas at Austin where she completed her doctorate in Educational Psychology with a specialty in School Psychology. She is licensed to practice in Texas, Massachusetts, and Arizona. Anne practiced school psychology in the Judson Independent School District in San Antonio, Texas before moving to Boston where she was the Director of the Learning Center for Dean College in Franklin, Massachusetts. She recently moved to Phoenix where she is coaching and practicing psychology. Anne still maintains her Boston connection where she is the Coach of the World TeamTennis Boston Lobsters and the mental training consultant for Harvard University's women's tennis team. She is a USPTA Pro 1 and a member of the Head/Penn Racquet Sports Speaker's Bureau.

Anne is playing on the women's tour again at the age of 46. She began her comeback in January 2005. After only nine tournaments, she has reached the semi-finals in doubles four times, and she won her first doubles tour title in June 2005 after being off of the tour for 14 years.

To contact Anne for further information about her books and video or to schedule her for a presentation to your team or company you may contact her by phone at 480-272-5085 or by email at anne@annesmithtennis.com.

Printed in the United States
77767LV00006B/613-624

9 780977 895809